COUNTDOWN TO GREATNESS

Greatness Lives Within You

Find It

Ignite It

Michael Carter Griffn

Not upside down, but transposed a bit and laid out backwards, yes this is how author Michael Carter Griffin organizes his chapters in *Countdown To Greatness – C2G Greatness Lives Within You Find It Ignite It*. Starting with the last chapter and finishing with his first, Griffin uses every variation of typesetting, font, various flowcharts and graphic tools at his disposal to imprint his truisms upon the reader in a unique style. This wordsmithing hedges on poetry, although the content is inherently within the self-help genre. Claiming to be a victim of having a short attention span, the whimsical and somewhat humorous depictions of the content is different from any other book I have read. It is fun, informative and definitely different.

He talks about the goals of humility when used with wisdom to be a very persuasive personal forte. The typical success pyramid is highlighted with more detail, and his book reads as if it were a *PowerPoint* presentation. He dedicates his book to himself – why? Because he feels you have never seen an author dedicate a book to himself – again, being out-of- the-box original in thoughts. I particularly enjoyed his thoughts on the subject of learning. He combines science and art as being the two important character traits to bestow knowledge upon oneself. He is "right-on" in my opinion, and it's effortless to read his charts and summations on this subject in his unusual way.

An author who emerges from a rather straightforward lifestyle, he uses his printed platform to bust out of the constraints of normality and challenges the status quo. This book would be best received as a printed version, as paging it will be half the fun of reading it, always being surprised by what lies ahead (or behind in his case). This is a great gift for young adults as well, as the rebellious formatting will encourage a new generation of authors to stray over the lines – and, not staying between the lines. It is original, fun and inspiring, and something I can simply say, "You have never seen anything like this." This is an ideal gift for a high-school graduating class as it will be as much fun ink on paper can possess. I highly recommend *Countdown To Greatness* to all those aspiring to be great in their own lives. An excellent book on how to live your life the best way you can. It will help guide you on determining what things really matter and your purpose in this journey called life.

- Pacific Book Review-

"Failure is not a negative; failure is part of the learning process, and helps to drive improvement."

Is there a blueprint to finding greatness in oneself? It is believed that to be great one only need to be positive and look in the mirror, as greatness is held within.

Griffin shows how basic principles of science and art lead to learning and finding a balance using repetition, practice, and refinement. Some individuals have learned the art of finding greatness within themselves, and others need a road map to guide them along the way. *Countdown to Greatness* encourages readers to reduce negativity and replace it with peace, self-worth, and positivity. By looking within one's own mind, they can learn self-esteem and a feeling of purpose. This leads to achieving greatness. Readers are encouraged to continuously improve and reinvent their creativity, thus leading to a better understanding of oneself.

Chapters are presented in reverse and intended as a countdown to assist the reader with a step-by-step guide to becoming a better person within. Written for those with short attention spans, the large print chapters are quick and to the point, offering simple instructions to find and ignite greatness. The writing style is playful and purposeful, guiding the reader to see life as a work in progress and strive to continue working on greatness. The author uses silly anecdotes to engage the reader to look deeper and ignite a desire for performance and a drive that leads to self-realization. The general takeaway is to follow your dreams, which will ultimately lead to the greatness that already lives inside you.

*- **The US Review of Books***

Introduction - Before we begin . . .

Please note 2 specific characteristics that make this book uniquely different.

1) Chapters are presented backwards.

(10,9,8,7,6,5,4,3,2,1,0) – a Countdown. Why? Because I want this book to be different that any book you have ever read. Seriously, how many books have you read that start with the last chapter? My guess = zero.

(Read the note below in the mirror.)

- ALWAYS REMEMBER -
READING BACKWARDS IS OK

2) Lots of wordz are mispaled on purpose! Why?

This is an oh-fishul bookuv wizdum! Werdz are miss-spaled en-tenshunullee, to help waik up your brane! I spale words funnetick-lee two! In uh-dishun, I like to mis-pronounciate words on porpoise.
I want yu to ekspeeree-ents the freedom of a yuneek vokab-you-larry – embraiced by the in-light-in-mint and ek-sight-ment of po-ten-shul mis-pro-nun-see-ashun! Ok – I admit – I'm a littul ex-in-trik! (I'm just kidding – this is the only page with a bunch of misspelled words.)

Haa-Hah!

Just for fun, my Top Ten random thoughts and quotes are provided below – they will help get your mind going. (Please note: this Top Ten list is mathematically 10% improved over other Top Ten lists. Can you figure out why this is the Best Top Ten Ever!? Hint: 10 + 1 =.)

1) There is no "ME" in TEAM (unless you spell "TEAM" backwards, and cross out the "A" and the "T").

    M A̶ E T̶ – you see what I mean?

2) I'm not OCD. (By the way, the term "OCD" is not in alphabetical order! Someone needs to fix that.)
3) Always finish what you . . .
4) Stop using acronyms – ASAP!
5) I can't remember the last time I forgot something.
6) A penny saved is only $999,999.99 away from $1 million.
7) _{Small writing is really annoying!}
8) Humility – one of my greatest qualities
9) On a scale of 1 to 10, how do you rate scales of 1 to 10?
10) Be decisive . . . or not. (Should this one be last? I can't decide.)
11) My train of thought has now left the station.

Table of Contents

Dedications	10: 1 - 5
Knowledge, Understanding And Wisdom	9: 1 - 4
The Secret to Learning	8: 1 - 4
Continuous Improvement	7: 1 - 4
Leadership And Teamwork	6: 1 - 4
The Zone	5: 1 - 4
The Moment	4: 1 - 4
True Freedom - The Art of Decision-Making	3: 1 - 4
GPS for Life	2: 1 - 4
All You!!!	1: 1 - 4
Be You!!!	0: 1 - 4

Every Challenge is an Opportunity

Chapter 10

Dedications

Believe In The Miracle You Already Are

Believe In The Miracle You Are Meant To Become

1) This book is dedicated to my wife – Cathy, and our two sons: Joshua & Jacob.

Thank you Cathy for your love and support. Thank you Josh and Jacob for being great sons and awesome young men, and for introducing new people to our family. Josh' wife Cara and Jacob's wife Taylor are great new additions. Plus Jacob's and Taylor's daughter Tilly and son Oliver are also part of our growing family. And yes - Grandchildren are so much fun!!!

Thank you all for being awesome and amazing …. AWESUMAZING! Yes -That's a word … I made it up.

2) This book is dedicated to my entire family, my friends, and the many people I worked with over the years.

Thank you for your inspiration.

3) This book is dedicated to all SAS Readers (<u>S</u>hort <u>A</u>ttention <u>S</u>pan).

I am a self-diagnosed SAS reader. For all of SAS, this is a short book with **BIG** words (**BIG** as in **PRINT SIZE**, not # of letters, like disestablishmentarianism). What kind of word is that anyway? Sounds like some kind of anti-government ice cream. "I'll have 2 scoops of disestablishmentarianism."

4) This book is dedicated to you - the individual reader, and to myself - the author.

Why? Because we're a Team. And I've never seen a book dedicated back to the reader and/or the author. What can I say? I like to be different.

Our purpose in life is to make the world a better place, and we can do that by making a positive difference in the lives of the people around us. This book is a simple guide to help us see our own potential, as well as the potential in others - giving us the opportunity to make a positive difference, and make our world a better place. Time to shine!

Special Dedication to Teachers and Protectors

To Teachers - Thank you for helping us learn to read, and helping us figure out how we can learn for ourselves; and thank you for helping us learn to believe in ourselves.

To Protectors - Military; Police/Sheriff; Fire/Rescue/Emergency Services; Healthcare - Thank you for protecting our families, our freedoms and our communities; and thank you for protecting our lives.

To Teachers and Protectors - You make the world a better place, by making a positive difference in the lives of the people around you. You are Heroes every single day, and a shining example of what "Countdown To Greatness" is all about.

Chapter 9

Knowledge, Understanding And Wisdom

Better Information =
Better Decisions =
Better Outcomes

Knowledge =

Awareness of facts and data about self, others and the world around us.

Understanding =

How our knowledge applies to self, others and the world around us.

Wisdom =

Applying our knowledge and our understanding to make positive impacts for others, which makes positive impacts for ourselves and the world around us.

Chapter 8

The Secret to Learning

Learning is the Perfect Combination of Science and Art.

LEARNING =

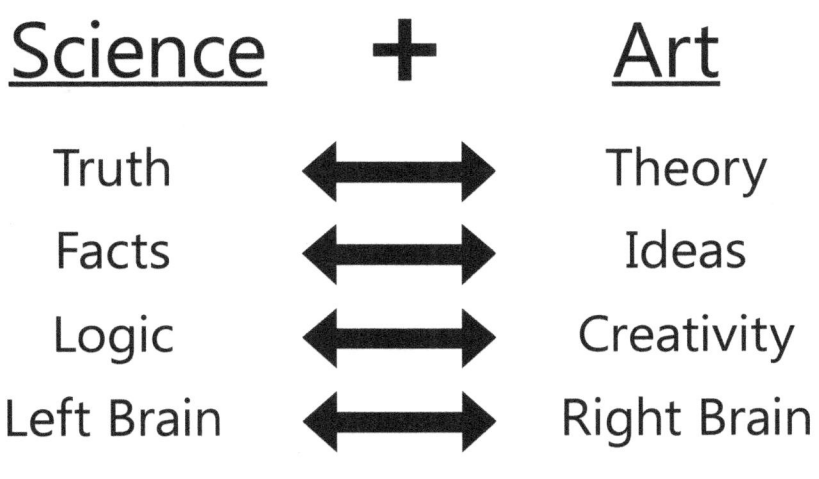

Find Your Balance.

The Learning Process =

1) Hear (repeat as necessary).
2) Read (repeat as necessary).
3) Do (repeat - repeat - repeat).
4) Make mistakes.

   a) Mistakes are learning opportunities (hidden opportunities, so make sure you're ready to accept them).

   b) Failure is <u>not</u> a negative; failure is part of the learning process, and helps to drive improvement.

Learning is Continuous

Repetition and Replication

Practice and Refinement

Enhanced Learning.

The Highest Form of Learning

Teaching Someone Else Your Skill/Talent

- Develops your proficiency.
- For your specific respective skill/talent, develops <u>your mastery</u>.

Chapter 7

Continuous Improvement

We Must Get Better to Be Better.
Greater Value and Effectiveness
is a Product of Higher Proficiency
(What you do) and Higher
Efficiency (How you do it).

Continuous improvement applies to individuals, teams and organizations.

Continuous Improvement Cycle

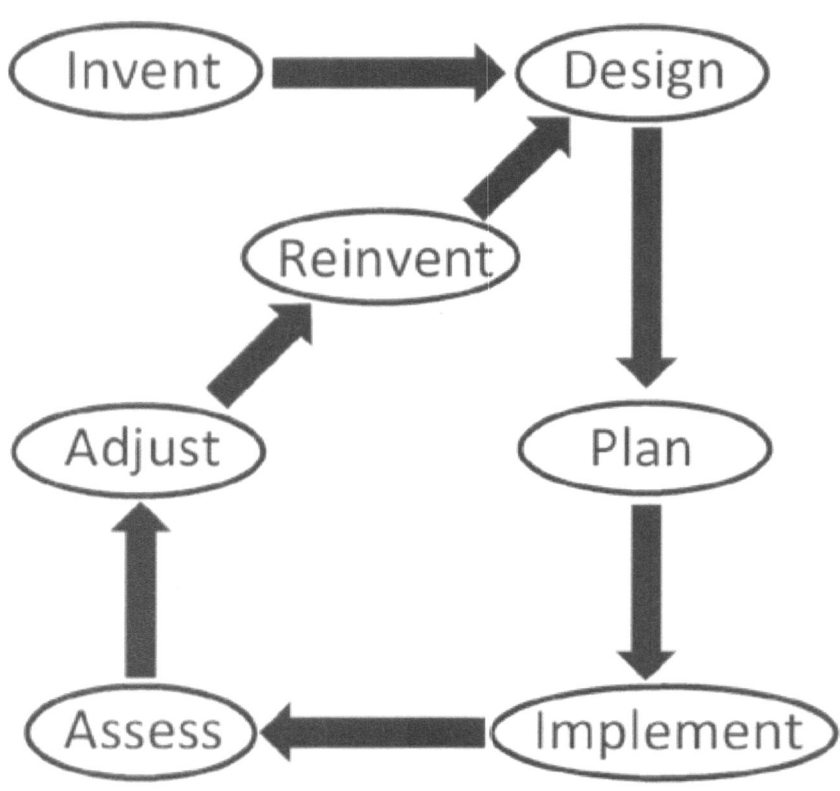

Focus on outcomes and added value, rather than compliance and regulation.

Continuous Improvement:

(Inspires Creativity)

Builds Stronger Individuals, Teams and Organizations.

- Stronger Planning
- Stronger Organization
- Stronger leadership

Applies to:

Expansion = More
Contraction = Less
Stabilization = Same

RESOURCES

Chapter 6

Leadership And Teamwork

Inspire Yourself by Inspiring Others!

Leadership Requires Character

- <u>I</u>ntegrity
- Commit<u>ment to</u> Excellence
- Genuine <u>Concern f</u>or Others

Leadership Requires Skills

- <u>C</u>ommuni<u>cation B</u>uilds Trust.
- <u>T</u>rust B<u>uilds Rela</u>tionships.
- <u>R</u>elation<u>ships L</u>ead to Team <u>Building.</u>
<u>CTR CTR CTR</u>

Team Building = TEAMWORK

TEAM – Problem Solving
TEAM – Respect
TEAM – Conflict Resolution
TEAM – Celebration
TEAM – Success

Positive Leadership:

- Drives Teamwork
- Encourages Creativity
- Recognizes and Supports Individual and Team Potential

Leadership Drives Individual and Team Achievement/Success.

- Motivation x Ability = Performance.
- Autonomy (freedom to make decisions) + Mastery (excelling at specific role) + Purpose (I'm making a positive difference.) = Drive *("Drive" by Daniel H. Pink)*.
- Performance + Drive, leads to reaching and redefining individual and team potential.
- Leadership and management are NOT the same. Lead people; manage process. (Process and procedure have minimal impact without the people to put them into place. Attempts to control/ manage people lead to false hope and individual/team frustration.)
- Know 1) when to lead; 2) when to let others lead; and 3) when to get out of the way so individuals and the team can excel.

Chapter 5

The Zone

Life is ALWAYS a
Work-In-Progress.

The Zone

Each level is dependent on reaching all previous levels. For example, we cannot reach level 2 without first reaching level 1; we cannot reach level 3 without first reaching levels 2 and 1; etc.

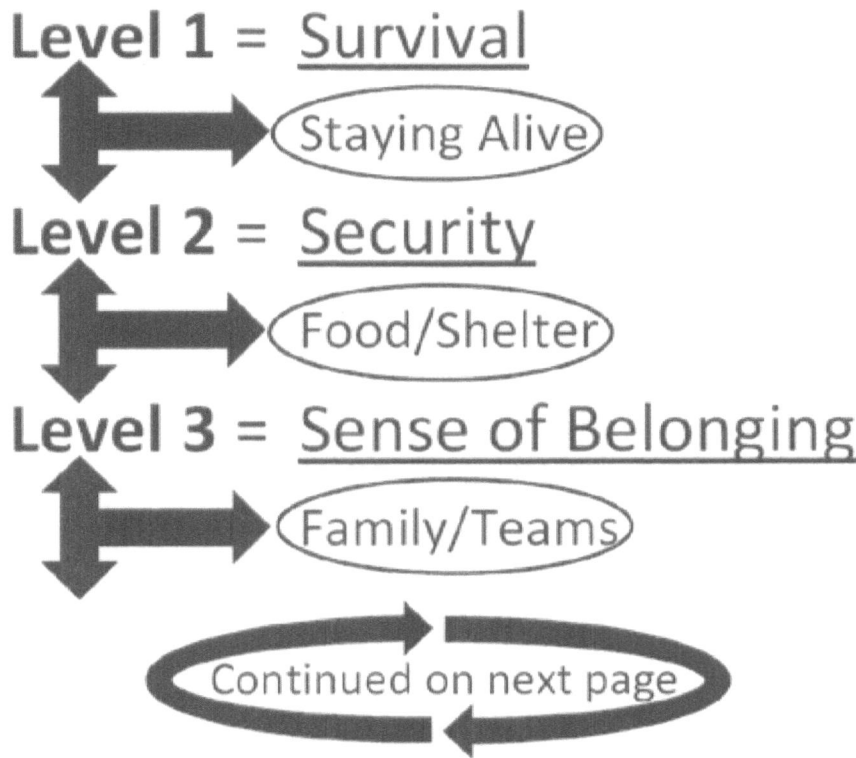

Level 1 = Survival — Staying Alive

Level 2 = Security — Food/Shelter

Level 3 = Sense of Belonging — Family/Teams

Continued on next page

The Zone, continued

Level 4 = <u>Self-Esteem</u>

The ZONE Pyramid

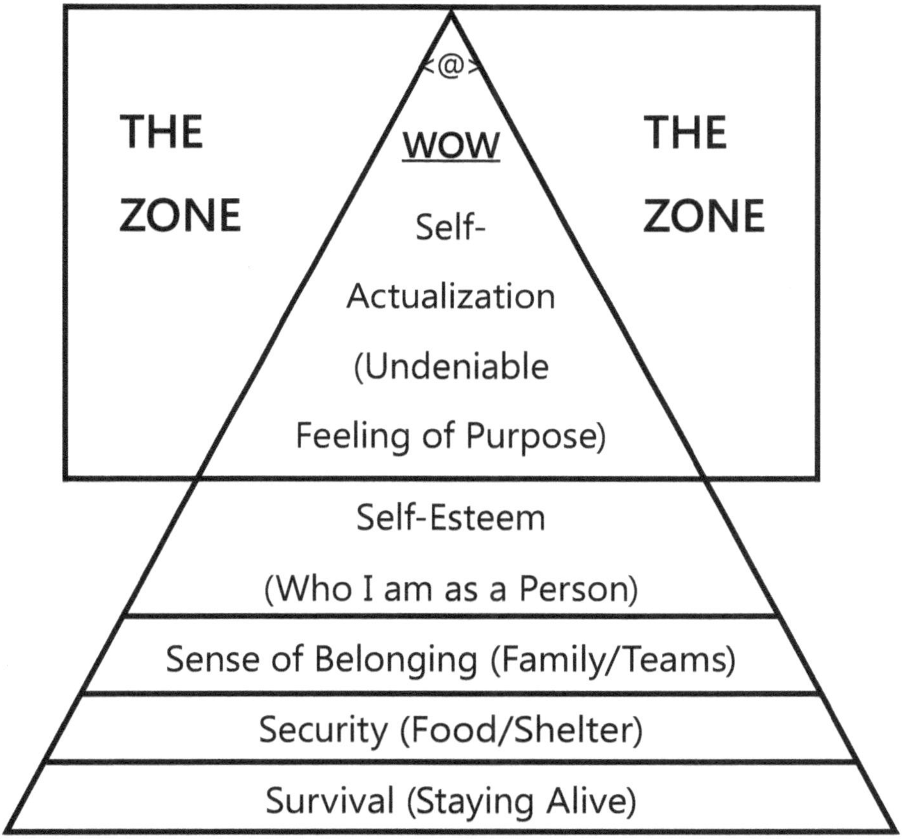

THE ZONE | **WOW** <@> | **THE ZONE**

Self-Actualization
(Undeniable Feeling of Purpose)

Self-Esteem
(Who I am as a Person)

Sense of Belonging (Family/Teams)

Security (Food/Shelter)

Survival (Staying Alive)

Chapter 4

The Moment

Seek Out Positives – in Yourself,

Others and the World.

You Will Always Find Positives,

as Long as You Are Looking for Them.

The Moment

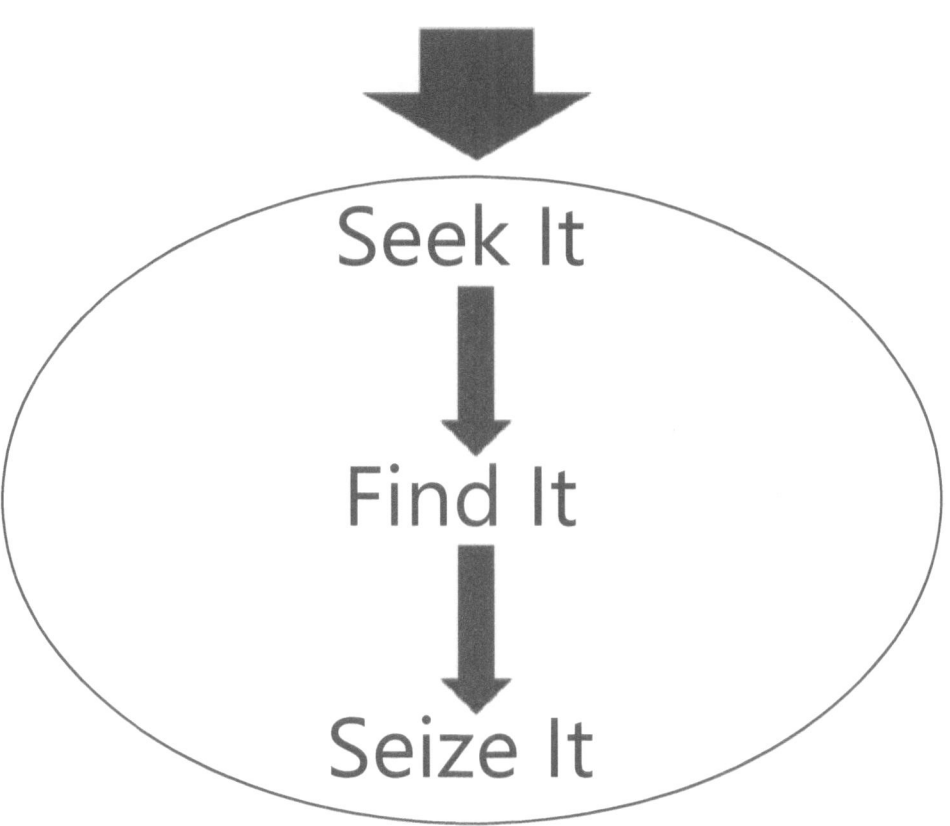

The Moment

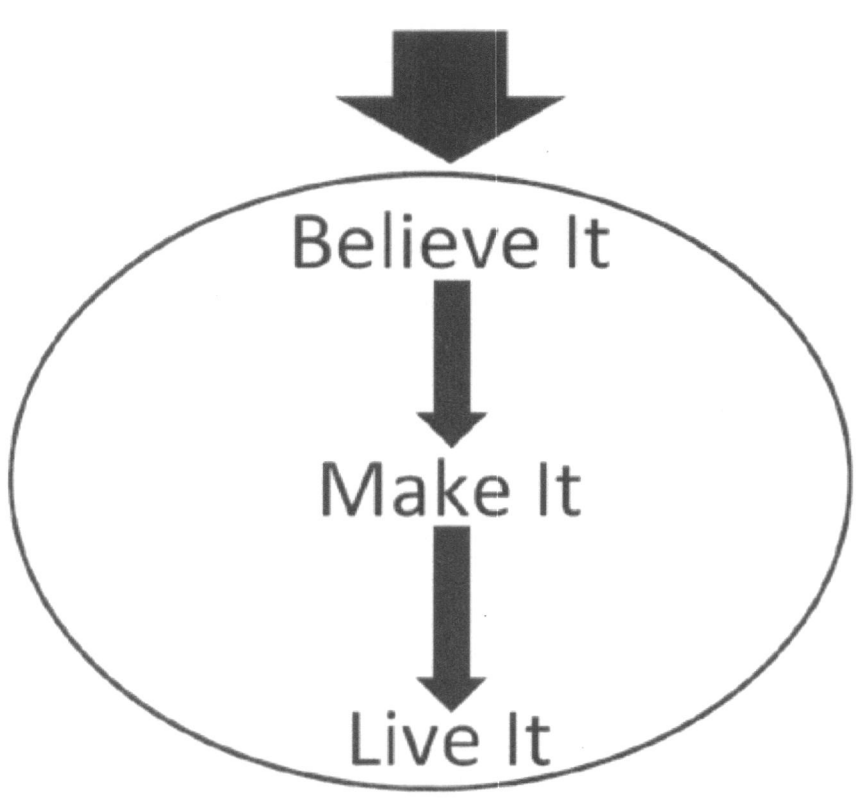

The Moment

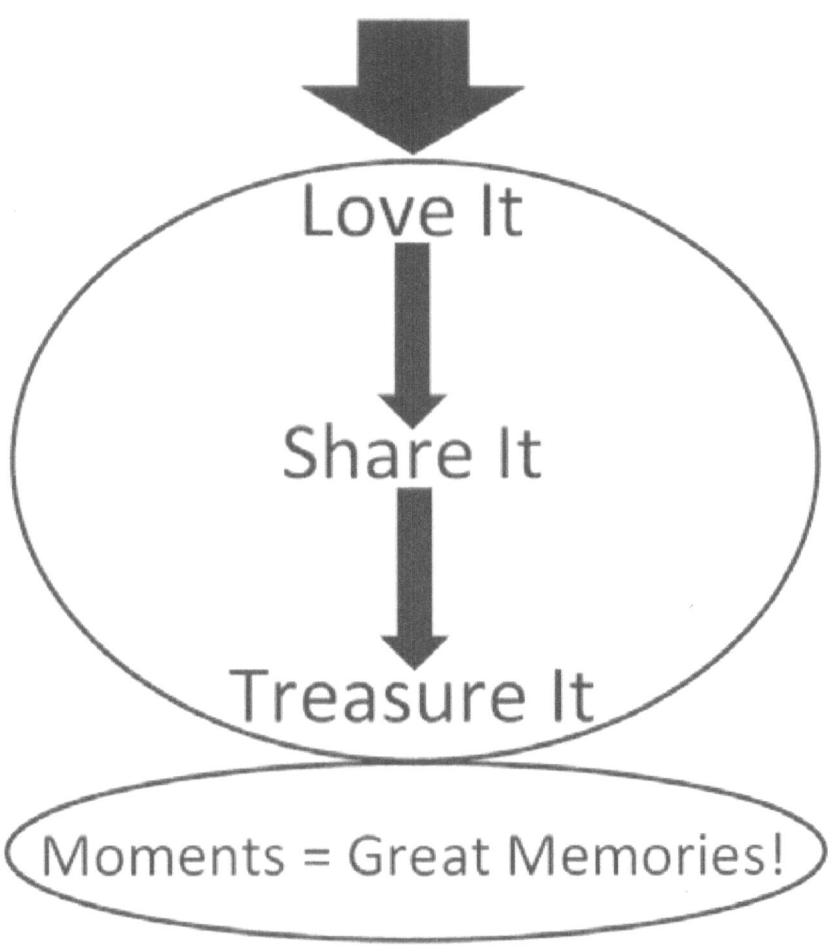

Chapter 3

True Freedom - The Art of Decision-Making

Erase Negativity.
Replace with Positivity.
Embrace the Freedom of
Faith, Hope and Love.

1 - Erase Negativity:

- Anger
- Guilt
- Fear

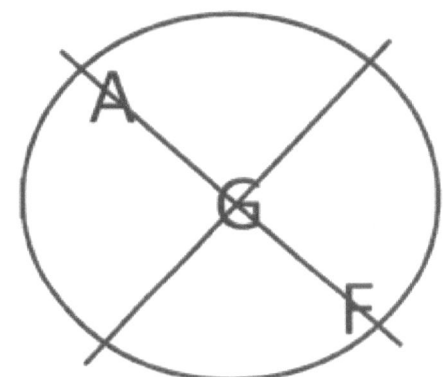

Focusing on these 3 can lead to negativity and bad decisions.

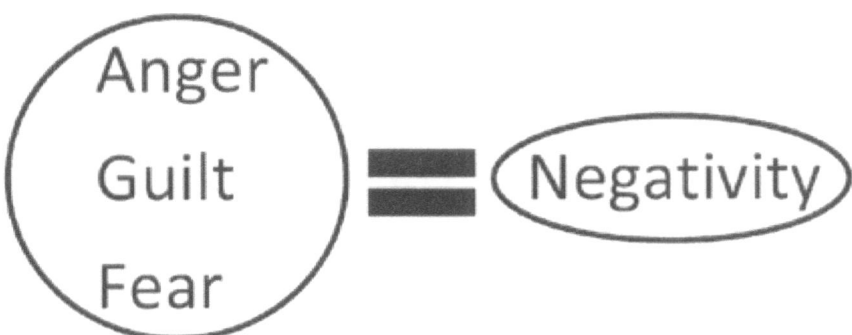

2 - Replace w/Positivity:

- **Anger** with **Peace**
- **Guilt** with **Self-worth**
- **Fear** with **Courage**

(Courage thru Adversity)

These 3 lead to positivity.

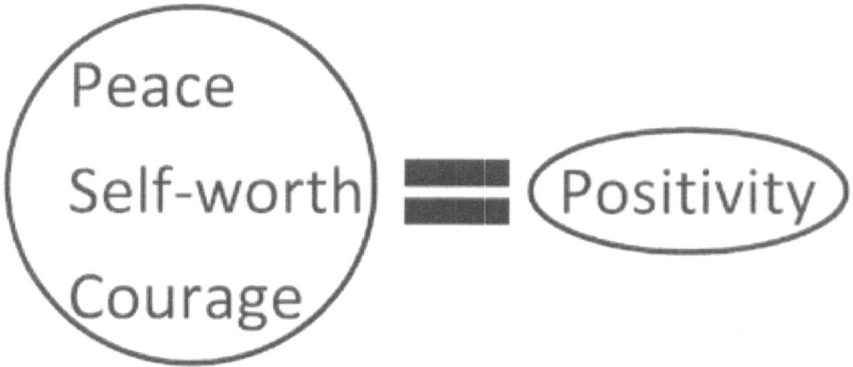

3 - Embrace Freedom.

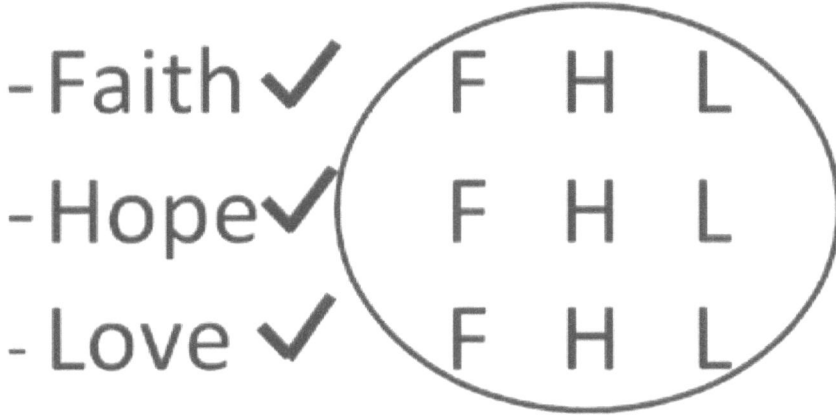

These 3 lead to true freedom and good decisions.

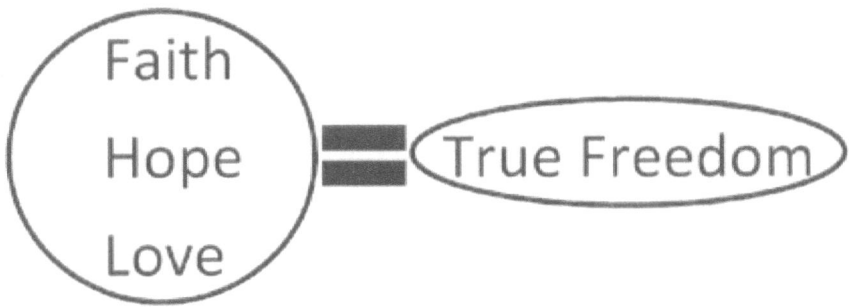

3 - 4

Chapter 2

GPS for Life

Short-Term Decisions are Easier,
Once You Define Your Focus
and Your Long-Term Goal.
Know Where You Want to Go,
and Turn on Your GPS.

Faith - GPS

Believe in **God**.

He Loves You and Believes in You.

Believe in **People**.

Love, Encourage and Support
Those around You.

Believe in **Self**.

You are **U**nique!
You are **S**pecial!
You are **A**mazing!

= **U S A**

Hope - GPS

Make the World
A Better Place.

For **God**
For **People**
For **Self**

True Inspiration Comes
From Inspiring Others!

Love - GPS

Love **God.**
Love **People.**
Love **Self.**

Love Who You Are and What You Do.

Love the Difference You Make Every Day in the Lives of The People Around You.

Erase Negativity; Replace w/Positivity; and Embrace the Freedom of Faith/Hope/Love. This Formula Leads to More Moments!

Chapter 1

ALL YOU!!!

"The Meaning of Life is to Find Your Gift. The Purpose of Life is to Give It Away."

Pablo Picasso

Today is Just the Beginning

Every Day is the First Day in the Rest of Your Life

Tomorrow will Soon be Yesterday - Make Today Count

Now is Your Time – Your Time is Now

You Have the GPS -

Find Faith

Find Hope

Find Love

The End of One Road is the Beginning of Another

Find Success in Your Journey -

Don't Stop Believin'

("Don't Stop Believin'" by Journey)

Seek Out and Make Moments;

Make Your Moments Count

Believe in Who You Are, and

Always Remember –

You are Loved to

INFINITY!

ALL YOU!!!

Chapter zero

<u>BE YOU!!!</u>

<u>BE</u>LIEVE IN <u>YOU</u>RSELF

———————

FOLLOW YOUR DREAMS

BE - The Positive

BE - The One

BE - The Miracle

BE - The Hope

BE - The Light

BE - The Strength

BE - The Difference

BE GREAT!

To Find Greatness, Look in the Mirror. Greatness is Staring Back at You!

Greatness is Waiting. Rise to Your Potential. Face Every Challenge.

BE GREAT!

10-9-8-7-6-5-4-3-2-1-

The Countdown to
Greatness is
Now Complete.
Time for You to

BLAST OFF and BE GREAT!

<u>BE YOU!!!</u>

Believe In The Miracle You Already Are

Believe In The Miracle You Are Meant To Become

Summary of "Countdown to Greatness"

"Countdown to Greatness" C2G is designed to ignite and re-ignite an individual's awareness of their potential. The book reminds us that all individuals have greatness within them, and we all have the ability to make a positive difference in the lives of others. By helping others, we help ourselves to become better individuals, and move closer and closer to own potential and our own greatness.

When we understand the internal emotional reward of helping others, we begin to see not only our potential as individuals, but also see our potential as members of a family, a team, or a group of individuals working together for a common purpose.

C2G provides basic principles of individual development, presented in a condensed and easy-to-understand format. Individuals of all ages can take the information and apply it in their daily lives. Readers can continuously look to C2G to remind them of **their** purpose, so they can find the key to **their** self-inspiration. Once we find our internal fire, we will always know how to rediscover our fire and re-ignite.

I wrote C2G to make a positive difference in the lives of others. I was inspired to write this book as a tribute to all those who have inspired me throughout my career and my life. My hope is that Countdown to Greatness will ignite that same type of inspiration in everyone that reads this book. And if reading this book inspires you, then you have inspired me even more, as inspiration is a continuous cycle.

We all have greatness within us. It is up to us to find it and share it with all those around us. Time to Inspire! Time to Be Great!

About the Author

Michael Carter Griffin was born on August 5, 1963, in Williamston, a small town in Eastern North Carolina. He is a 1985 accounting graduate of Liberty University in Virginia. He took his accounting degree to Pinehurst, NC and his first job in a regional accounting firm. In 1987, he was hired as Chief Finance Officer (CFO) for Moore County Government in Carthage, NC. During his 17-year service with the county, he obtained his CPA certificate, as well as various designations and certifications as a public finance officer and a local government leader. He then worked for the private sector for three years as CFO for Pine Needles and Mid Pines Resorts in Southern Pines, NC. In 2007, he returned to public service as CFO for Moore County Schools, also in Carthage, until his retirement in December 2015. He retired after a 30-year career. He and his wife Cathy have 2 sons, Joshua and Jacob.

www.ingramcontent.com/pod-product-compliance
Lightning Source LLC
Chambersburg PA
CBHW021431070526
44577CB00001B/166